POUR TOI
by
KRISTINA NIVEN

Paintings by
Fiona Owen

THE MEDICI SOCIETY LTD.
LONDON

The edition is limited to
1050
copies
of which one thousand are for sale

Copy number

Printed in England
ISBN 0 85503 084 4

To my father,

the man I will

always love

The sea is a mystery
In this mysterious world of today.
When we see those boats leak,
We think.

Daniel mon miel!
Tu me caresses si bien.
J'ai envie d'être au ciel.
Je t'aime toi et les tiens.
Oh! Comme je t'aime Daniel.

One hears, but one forgets.
One sees and realises.
Time flies by.

One speaks, sometimes mumbles.
One flitters then touches.
Time flies by.

One smells and likes.
One feels and loves.
Time flies by.

FIONA OWEN

Les jours passent et plus les nuits
Deviennent profondes.
Y a-t-il une raison qui puisse
Expliquer mon Soleil
Vingt-quatre heures sur vingt-quatre?
C'est peut-être TOI . . . . . .

L'Amour, l'amitié et la sincérité
Se lit sur une rose rouge.

Everything is quiet
Whilst my heart is burning
Just like the red candle on the table.

FIONA OWEN

Les journées sont longues,
Tu me manques tant,
Même les secondes sont infernales;
Mais sont pourtant plus courtes,
Puisque mes rêves sont remplis de . . .
Toi.

Evenings go by, days go by.
There has never been a full stop.

Minutes disappear, and seconds vanish.
Will there ever be a full stop?

These are just small memories, flashes.
When will there be a full stop?

Quelle joie de t'avoir rencontré.
Quel plaisir de te connaître.
Et quel bonheur de te connaître
Encore . . .

FIONA · OWEN · 1984

Blowing you all my new-born wishes
On a lovely spring day . . .

Sending you all my love
In a colourful way,
So that I can
Brighten up your day.

Toi . . .
Tu éclaircis mon passage
Et rembellis la lumière
Chaque fois que je passe devant toi.

Our love
Our trust
Our beliefs

Link us together

Les reflets des lumières sur le lac
La nuit, ressemblent à une chaîne d'or
Qui brille sans raison,
Une beauté imaginaire que . . .
Personne ne comprendra.

To show a smile
And share a little love
Are the first signs of friendship.

J'ai envie d'être contente
Juste une fois dans ma vie.
Je te prie mon chéri
Satisfais mon envie.

Kristina Niven was born in Geneva and lived in Château-d'Oex in Switzerland and in the South of France. During her early childhood she greatly enjoyed accompanying her parents on their many trips abroad. She was educated in Lausanne until the age of eighteen, after which she attended a Sotheby's course in London and also pursued her interest in languages. She is now occupied in redecorating the house she lives in on the Côte d'Azur.

Kristina Niven est née à Genève et a vécu à Château-d'Oex en Suisse, ainsi que sur la Côte d'Azur. Durant son enfance, elle a eu grand plaisir à accompagner ses parents dans leur nombreux voyages à l'étranger. Elle a fait ses études à Lausanne jusqu'à l'âge de dix-huit ans, et suivi par la suite des cours à Sotheby's à Londres tout en étudiant les langues étrangères. A l'heure actuelle, Kristina s'occupe à redécorer la maison qu'elle habite sur la Côte d'Azur.

Fiona Owen was born in Wales in 1957. After obtaining her B.A. Hons degree in illustration in 1978, she settled in the Cotswolds with her artist husband to take up a full time career in painting. Her beautifully intricate work is inspired by Medieval illuminated manuscripts, such as *Les Très Riches Heures du Duc de Berry*. She has had several successful exhibitions in London and her work is collected world-wide.